BURCHILL ON BECKHAM

BURCHILL ON

BECKHAM

Julie Burchill

Published by Yellow Jersey Press 2001

2 4 6 8 10 9 7 5 3 1

Copyright © Julie Burchill 2001

Julie Burchill has asserted her right under the
Copyright, Designs and Patents Act 1988 to be identified as
the author of this work

First published in Great Britain in 2001 by
Yellow Jersey Press
Random House, 20 Vauxhall Bridge Road,
London SW1V 2SA

Random House Australia (Pty) Limited
20 Alfred Street, Milsons Point, Sydney,
New South Wales 2061, Australia

Random House New Zealand Limited
18 Poland Road, Glenfield,
Auckland 10, New Zealand

Random House (Pty) Limited
Endulini, 5A Jubilee Road, Parktown 2193, South Africa

The Random House Group Limited Reg. No. 954009
www.randomhouse.co.uk

A CIP catalogue record for this book
is available from the British Library

ISBN 0-224-06291-7

Papers used by The Random House Group Limited are
natural, recyclable products made from wood grown in
sustainable forests; the manufacturing processes conform
to the environmental regulations of the country of origin

Printed and bound in Great Britain by
Mackays of Chatham plc, Chatham, Kent

For Stuart Walton

CONTENTS

PROLOGUE:

Who Do You Think You Are?

A wise man once said that satire died the day Henry Kissinger received the Nobel Peace Prize. But for me, satire finally pegged it on that spring day in 2001 when it was announced that Coutts & Co, the royal bank, were to open a special department to court the boy kings of football. Even before it opened for business, some 60 players had signed up.

What space odyssey had led us to these strange days, in this parallel universe, where the Queen's bank danced attendance on young men it would previously not have employed as doormen? At first it seemed like some sort of sarky joke, like that annual day at the major public school when the masters wait on the pupils, and call them 'Sir' in horrible oily drawls. But the royal bank meant business; a spokesperson said, 'There was a time when footballers were known for wasting all their money and ending their careers bankrupt. But all that is in the past; they are much more sensible now ... There's been a huge influx of money to the game over the last eight years and there's never been a better time for them to manage their money properly ... They only have about twelve years in their career at the top and we have to ensure they make the most of that.'

All this sounded fine – New Britain, New Money, breaking down the fusty old barriers of privilege, all that jazz – until one remembered that Coutts itself had recently been the subject of much loose talk. It was alleged that such stellar clients as Andrew Lloyd Webber and Phil Collins had closed their accounts and taken their pennies home in a huff. Fancy – finishing up the stuff left on the side of the plate by characters as irretrievably naff as Phil Collins and Andrew Lloyd Webber! Was this really, then, the New Breed of switched-on, stylish footballer who would take the Beautiful Game for ever out of the sweaty slipstreams of naffness and into the deep blue depths of Cool? Or was the account at Coutts just the latest in a long line of footie follies like mock-Tudor houses, plastic Alice bands worn on the pitch, 'opening a boutique, Brian' and sleeping with Page 3 girls who had higher IQs than you?

The weird, sad thing about English football is that only when players were paid pocket money did they seem like real men; the minute they got a man's wage, they became Lads; then, when they achieved a king's ransom, they became little boys. Many of us were mildly surprised when we discovered that one of David Beckham's hobbies was tracing and copying cartoon drawings such as *The Lion King* – which he would send to his fiancée Victoria Adams as love tokens – but we soon got used to the idea, and probably thought 'Ah, isn't that sweet.' The same with the revelation, made to Michael Parkinson on his television chat show, that he first worked out Victoria fancied him 'when she bought me a big bunny, and I think that was the first time I realised she liked me a little bit.'

But we weren't really shocked, as we would have been if we'd learned this about Stanley Matthews. By this time, we knew that the heartbreakingly named George Best had for three decades been so addicted to the bottomless bottle that he would apparently rather die than stop suckling at its toxic teat, and that Tony Adams had regularly been so out of control on drink that he wet himself. We took to the idea of sportsmen as the new rock stars – drunken, drugged, destructive towards both themselves and their sexy blonde companions – with surprising equanimity. It came as a real relief to find out that tracing lions and taking receipt of large stuffed rabbits was as bad as it got with the boy Beckham.

Somehow, it made sense; there was a sort of folk memory which understood that once sportsmen stopped playing for the love of the game, things would go horribly wrong. For sport is basically playing, as children play; if this side of a human being is overly concentrated on, obviously everything else will be neglected. By being paid so little, Matthews and his contemporaries somehow brought dignity to the state of being a sportsman; that is, being able to run fast, kick a ball and generally skive off all the boring, soul-grinding, back-breaking jobs that other working-class men had to do. But obviously once huge amounts of money were awarded to adult men for not growing up, they were going to regress even further; it was the pure logic of the playpen.

Once we had Busby's Babes, and we were proud of them; from the Nineties onwards we had Britain's Amazing Footballing Babies, and we hung our heads in shame. They might be physically incontinent, like Adams, or simply emotionally and morally incontinent like Paul Gascoigne and Stan Collymore, but the end result is the same; generally, our footballers are a greater source of shame than pride to us, and have been for many years. And it is hard to believe that the vile behaviour of English players off the pitch is not reflected in the notoriously violent behaviour of England fans abroad, and vice versa; that overpaid players and underclass supporters alike are intent on playing out some sort of *danse macabre* amid the ruins of brute masculinity, determined to take as many as they can down with them. It is very hard, seeing footage of rioting England fans in the cities of mainland Europe, not to remember the last time large numbers of young English men were over there: to liberate Europe from Fascism. At the risk of sounding like a *Daily Mail* editorial – what went wrong?

David Beckham bears a great burden on his beautiful shoulders. While being the most perfectly childlike of modern footballers, and also the most fragrantly feminine, he is paradoxically the one to whom we look to return the once-beautiful game to that state of grace, that short-back-and-sides manly sainthood embodied by Matthews and Finney. Serious-eyed, resplendently saronged, perfectly still, wearing his wife's knickers, this holy fool makes clowns of his contemporaries when he effortlessly equates football with civility while answering Michael Parkinson's question: 'Football is a very laddish game and very macho. Here you are, you're not a boozer and you don't go around thumping your wife, you adore your child and you're this gay icon. That doesn't embarrass you, does it?'

'No, not at all.'

'And you talk in your book about this feminine side that you like and admire. You're against the grain —'

'I think it's because I've never been involved in that sort of circle. When I was younger, I used to stay at home and watch *Match of the Day* instead of going down to the corner shop for a bottle of cider. That's the way I've been brought up. I have a drink now and again, but I don't go out drinking and beating up women, so I'm happy.'

And this is the key: rich, successful and sexy, Beckham is, above all, happy, in an age where flagrant displays of happiness are frowned on by the rich and famous. Every last whinging celeb has a customised sob story about how they saw

Mommy kissing Santa Claus when they were five years old, and that's why they're a dipsomaniac/nymphomaniac /bulimic/alcoholic. Being happy is seen as shallow, a sign of peasant breeding; to be 'troubled', on the other hand, is classy, deep, fascinating. But the sad fact is that it is neurotic people who are shocking bores. Like junkies, they all have exactly the same personality. Transpose interviews with Geri Halliwell, Robbie Williams and Tara Palmer-Tomkinson, for instance, and you'll never be able to tell who's saying what.

Beckham has bypassed this sad attention-seeking, as he has bypassed the Crisis of Masculinity, the End of Industry and the failure of *The Lion King II* to do the business at the box office. Does this make him really dumb, very clever or just extremely fortunate? No one is sure. And whether he can take English football with him, under his captainship, out from the darkness and into the light, remains to be seen. But if not him, then who, and if not now, when?

CHAPTER ONE

Wannabe

There is something very poignant about photographs of the famous before they became so. The obvious tear-jerkers are the ones of the ugly ducklings who became supermodel swans. But the real heart-breakers are those of the beautiful young famous when they were even younger and more beautiful, yet strangers to themselves, raw and itchy in their own skins. ('Mum, I'm scared! Is it shingles?' 'No, dear, it's nothing to worry about, you're just going to become a universal love icon who tastes every known pleasure but ultimately finds life meaningless and without value. Now go back to sleep.') They seem unsure as to why they don't feel normal, but also confident that the fame process will eventually explain them to themselves.

Of course, with hindsight we read into them that which was never there. Looking at the many photographs of the adolescent Diana Spencer, for example, it is tempting to take her ceaseless solemnity, her full-on melancholic stare, as a comment on what was to happen to her; that the twelve-year-old Diana is so sad because she, like the rest of us, has seen the Diana Spencer Story played out in pictures until its very end; 'And wasn't it a shame, how young I died . . .'

The pictures from the first professional photo session that the young David Beckham submitted himself to are extraordinary. Aged 21, in 1995, he is still living in lodgings in Salford while being trained up by Manchester United. (Odd that the ultimate sunshine boy should be inextricably bound to Britain's legendary city of rain.) He looks not shy, as might be expected, but shifty, as though he is there under false pretences. With his blond quiff, smooth skin and uncharacteristic greatcoat – well, it was Manchester – he sometimes looks at the camera as if calculating how soon he can get hold of it and destroy the evidence. At other times he has a barely suppressed smile, as though he and the cameraman are complicit in the understanding that this is not yet 'David Beckham' we see, and that there is an element of deceit in selling the photographs as such, but that, hey, he's game. The final portrait is almost creepy; Beckham sits on a pavement in jeans and black jacket, the words THE FINEST spray-canned on to the wall behind him. Here at last the crafty impostor smirk is gone, and Beckham has true Diana-faced gravitas; it's as though he's thinking (Obi Wan Kenobi voice) 'And so it came to be.' Go back even further, and all the clues are there; the ten-year-old Beckham wild-eyed beneath an England scarf, or the growing teenager posing in a different Manchester United strip each year, always a gift from his father. Such random snaps from nowhere can easily be corralled by the lazy writer into the back pages of a life destined for limelight – and would you deny me such small pleasures? – and of course one could find the same evidence in the family photograph albums of one-time playground heroes who went on to become bank clerks, drag queens and drolls. But there really does appear to have been something different about the boy Beckham from the word go; his strange, distant Joan of Arc eyes imply that, like her, he might well have even heard voices – except that they were the voices of Jimmy Hill, Brian Moore, 'The Saint' and Greavsie.

Football halfway through the Seventies, when David Beckham was born, was a strange beast. It had long lost the manly, love-of-the-game purity that we mope over in those old sepia photographs, but it was still far from being the Met Bar millionaire's lark it is today. In 1961 the same Jimmy Hill – the BHS Beelzebub of British TV sport – had been a professional player (Brentford and Fulham) and leader of the Professional Footballers' Union when he achieved the abolition of the players' maximum wage – around £12 a week at the time of Tom Finney and Stanley Matthews – and it immediately shot up to around £500 for the best players. By the late Sixties and the coming of the Western cultural revolution to the nation's urban hotspots (which by the time it got to England had basically boiled down to kipper ties and shagging for all), footballers were young, rich and dumb enough to enjoy all the pleasures that came with the breaking-down of deference, repression and tradition, and working-class enough not to have the safety net that was always there for middle-class hippies when they'd taken one trip too many.

Footballers, previously Men to a boy, became Lads. Increased leisure and affluence among the working class meant that, by the late Sixties – after ROSLA but before AIDS – young men didn't have to grow up as quickly as their fathers had. There could be a period between leaving school and getting married when, once you'd clocked off, you did little more for five years than drink, dance, pull and go to the football. The Seventies were when every Lad finally got his leg over, and they were everywhere, in all their feather-cut glory. Turn on the TV and there was Richard O'Sullivan in *Man About The House,* with his bra-and-suspenders plastic apron; every boy bar Dennis and the 'Mummy's little soldier' one in *Please Sir!* was at it; then there was Adam

Faith's Budgie, too thick to understand that it wasn't easy to do a runner in clogs. There were the great Lad pop stars: Rod Stewart, Ian Hunter, Phil Lynott, David Essex. Laugh-a-minute Lads like Jim Davidson. And even Lad lags: Ronnie Biggs, Johnny Bindon.

And there were sporting Lads: Barry Sheene, James Hunt. Malcolm Allison, who actually left his wife for 'Bunny Serena', was an early Elder Statesman of Lad. There were Lads wherever you looked. But Lad-dom, basically being about pissing it all away, only twice produced anything approaching greatness. And they were Tom Jones and George Best.

Both men, though coming to fame in the Sixties, only came into their own (and everybody else's) in the Seventies. They did all the things that Junior League Lads dreamed of in their wildest, wettest dreams: fathered boy children, knew that they could lick any girl in the room when they walked into Tramp, wore trousers that were truly an offence against theology and geometry. Above all, these Celtic princes drank for Wales and Ireland respectively. For Jones, this wasn't such a problem; famous for his gravely voice and somewhat overblown physique, drink only made him growlier and jowlier – though even he languished in lush Las Vegas obscurity for a decade or two before knocking himself back into shape and becoming, at last, an icon of cool. For Best, as an athlete, it was a tragedy – made even more so, and all the more self-perpetuating, by the fact that his beloved, shy mother also became an alcoholic in the process of dealing with the pressure of his fame, and subsequently died of drink. If Best had no good reason to drink himself into oblivion when he began, he certainly does now.

But back then, on the cusp of the Sixties and Seventies – that brief shimmering moment when, for the young working class, life did literally seem to be a dream – the Best effect was similar to the way that a generation of literary hopefuls had seen their dreams wash up on the rocks in their dirty glasses at the stained tables of Fitzrovia. Like young would-be poets who noted that Brendan Behan and Dylan Thomas were poets who drank, and who went on themselves to be drunks who wrote poems, young footballers started to grow their hair long like Best ('The Fifth Beatle'), date bosomy blondes like Best and worst, drink like Best.

Of course, they became a generation of walking wounded. A cautionary feature in the *Daily Mail* in February 2001 screamed DOWNFALL UNITED – 'They were the David Beckhams of their day. So how did these footballers end up destroyed by alcohol, women and gambling?' How indeed? Alan Hudson, for instance, was a hooded-eyed, lush-

locked young beauty when he joined
Chelsea (of course) at 17. 'Being a player
in the Sixties and Seventies was fantastic
fun,' he told the *Mail*. 'We were all
young, we followed the fashion scene
with a vengeance and we were friends
with pop stars. Life was far from boring.'
Ominously he adds: 'There really was
nothing better than playing a great game,
then going out for drinks and a good meal
. . . we used to go out to all the best bars
and clubs, where women would make a
beeline for us. At training in the morning,
you could always tell the players who
hadn't been home the night before,
because they'd turn up in the same
clothes, reeking of alcohol.' Hilariously,
highlighting the unconscious homo-
erotica of 'The Beautiful Game' (a
uniquely effete description; imagine
cricket being called by its aficionados
'The Radiant Play', or rugby 'The
Gorgeous Ruck'), which would end up
with millions of men screaming with

hatred at Victoria Beckham that she had the very sort of sex with her husband that they so wished he would give them ('POSH SPICE TAKES IT UP THE ARSE!'), Hudson went on to reflect, 'There were always women around, although I was more of a man's man and preferred drinking with my mates.' Inevitably, 'I was very easily led and was forever out on drinking binges that some-times lasted days.'

Interestingly, Hudson claims only to have earned £25 a week, playing for a First Division club in the Seventies; nevertheless, he married a blonde model (like Best), losing her to America in the harsh light of the Eighties (as Best did his Angie). Like Best, Hudson played 'soccer' in America, which is probably as low as any English player can go, literally; Tony Adams is still a well-respected man after regularly soiling himself, but playing for Seattle would have rendered him completely untouchable. At 49, Hudson lives with his mother, and writing for the *Sporting Life* means he no longer lives on the breadline as he did for most of the Nineties.

In the same feature, 52-year-old Stan Bowles – three wives and four children later, trumping Hudson's two-three – was found living with his mother, too. It is sad and strange but entirely understandable that these haggard, haunted ex-golden boys end up back with their mums, having stopped still mentally at the age when they were first discovered in all their tousle-haired, scabby-kneed glory. By 1983, Bowles was downing a bottle of vodka and eighty cigarettes a day, his body not so much his temple as his mangy old lock-up with the windows boarded over and the roof stoved in. One morning he drank so much that he thought he was having a heart attack and took himself off to hospital for treatment. The doctors took one look at him and put him into a psychiatric ward filled with, in Stan's words, 'schizophrenics and manic depressives'. He stayed there for five days; 'One man kept calling me his son; another kept telling me he had a train to catch . . . it was terrifying and made me realise how close I was to self-destruction.' It would be nice to think that one or both of the poor men mentioned also gave up the demon drink after the horrific experience of being incarcerated with a lunatic who kept insisting that he was Stan Bowles.

Malcolm MacDonald – 'Supermac', two wives, seven children – has managed to avoid going home to Mother, despite being forced to retire from football at the tender age of 29. Going to Fulham in 1968, at the age of 18, MacDonald predictably 'took to the high life like a duck to water . . . there was a real brashness about the game then,' he bitches, 'and a sense of freedom generally. Today's players may earn vast amounts, but they are owned by the marketing machines.' Back on form, old MacDonald has a boast: 'I was earning £500 a week and getting mobbed wherever I went. Footballers were the new pop stars and it was all long hair, flares and platform shoes. I did drink and smoke,' he swaggers, 'but that wasn't unusual. Because I was young and fit, I could down pint after pint and not feel the effects the next day.' So young and fit, in fact, that he had to retire at 29 with an arthritic knee! The pain of which, coincidentally, gave him a good excuse to down a bottle of whisky a day when 'the painkillers didn't work'.

Peter Marinello was the prettiest star of all, though; I remember having a moderate crush on him myself when I was ten and he signed to Arsenal in 1970, at the age of 19. Within days, the boy from an Edinburgh prefab was offered a guest appearance on *Top of the Pops* (a big deal back then), modelling contracts and newspaper columns. Being paid around £1,400 a week, he told the *Mail*, 'sustained a lifestyle of going out drinking with my team-mates until 3 a.m. Yet we always managed to make training – even if we did reek of booze.' (We've been here before, haven't we?) Bankrupt, unemployed and on benefits, still married to his childhood girlfriend, Marinello nevertheless reveals a nature as sweet as his teenage face: 'Of course I would love to be one of today's players, earning those vast sums of money. They only have to work for a couple of years and they're set up for life, whereas we had to make a 15-year career out of it to do that. I spend a lot of time at home with my wife, who hasn't been well. I may be relying on benefits, but I'm quite happy these days.'

These were the broken boughs of working-class British manhood who cast their battered shadow over the childhood of David Beckham. As he learned to walk and talk, they had a certain style, after a fashion; they were healthy, high-spirited young beasts, which is never without its charm unless you live next door to it. But frankly, they were always somewhat preposterous, in their three-piece suits, matching ties and clashing cravats, forever peeking cheekily out from under deep fringes. The trouble was that they all appeared to have based their act on that of Jack Wild as the Artful Dodger in *Oliver!*, a popular film of the time, ignoring the fact that he was about 12 years old. Thus, they were totally lacking in anything approaching dignity – that which the fortunate athlete has in lieu of brains.

And even on the frivolous front – hmm, the new pop stars? The friends of pop stars? What pop stars would these have been, precisely? Brian Poole and the Tremoloes? Marmalade? Whatever, the idea of even George Best marrying one of the ace face poptresses of the day – Marianne Faithfull, say – is unthinkable. He had Miss Worlds instead; today, it's very likely that a really top-class footballer wouldn't date a Miss World, believing it to be naff. They'd be saving themselves for a pop princess. You might shag a Jordan when you were half-cut, but you'd laugh about it with your mates afterwards, and you'd hold out for a Louise when it came to marriage. Like banking with Coutts, suddenly these barely educated little guttersnipes 'instinctively knew what was right', to quote the old sherry ad.

One of the main differences between footballers then and footballers now is that, right up to the late Eighties and the leaping Pentecostal flame of the rave culture, working-class Lads have generally been very suspicious of drugs, associating them with feebleness, poshness and the generally awful business of becoming a 'junkie'. (When I was growing up in early Seventies Bristol, so successful was anti-drug propaganda among my working-class compadres that even the rumour that someone had taken a puff of marijuana would invariably be met with a shudder, a shove and a cry of 'Ugh! Junkie!' from the hard boys and cool girls.) As Tom Jones memorably and hysterically once put it: 'Nobody wants to fight, not for his woman, not for his country. They all want the easy way. That's what is wrong with drugs. It takes a man to drink liquor. See, you can get high smoking pot and never get sick. But it takes a man to be able to hold his liquor – or be able to pay the penalty.'

Which just about makes alcohol the worst possible drug of choice for any athlete. All those calories, all those hangovers, all those riotous rucks! Whereas an illegal drug habit would, by necessity, have to be conducted with some discretion and circumspection, and would make a considerable impact on one's pocket, alcoholism is easily entered into and then easily maintained for years without anyone being aware of anything more sinister than so-and-so 'liking a bevvy' or 'reeking of booze'. Why footballers in particular are so susceptible to drink is an interesting question. Why don't we habitually witness the Titans of Wimbledon three sheets to the wind (probably because they tend to be American, actually; i.e. girls) or watch rugby players struggling to outdo their fans in the incontinence stakes? Is it because, with soccer, you can hide at the back, sloping off like a bookish schoolboy when you've got a filthy hangover? Is it the Boys' Club mentality? (If so, why isn't it such a problem for rugby players, whose sport is far more blokish and whose supporters just as drunken, in a more good-natured, not-with-ladies-present way, as football fans?)

I've said it before and I'll say it again, there is something far more homoerotic about football than there is about other sports. 'The Beautiful Game'; the sumptuously camp 'Three Lions' – 'Thirty years of hurt/ Never stopped me dreaming' indeed! (You sensitive little flower, you! Try to imagine the same sort of song about rugby or baseball!) Footballers do tend to be far better-looking than other sportsmen, and those little shorts show their legs off a treat; you couldn't blame any of the boys for sneaking a quick peek in the steam of the showers after the big game. And in many cases, excessive drinking is a sure sign of repressed homosexuality.

But it could be something sadder, less smutty that leads footballers to take refuge in the bottle – which is that they are, basically, treated as dumb hunks of meat, dazzling beasts, bought and sold on the market like things. Okay, they're handsomely rewarded, and it would look a bit off if they complained. But, regardless of who is to blame, footballers are definitely thought to be the stupidest of sportsmen; 'It just came at me and I hit it, Brian', over the moon, sick parrots, the lot.

Think about it. Golfers are given all sorts of Zen points (despite their startling and outlandish clothing), cricketers treated as guardians of national gravitas (even though they throw matches as enthusiastically as they throw balls) and tennis players are regarded as modern Olympians (never mind that they are the last species on earth to be impressed by what used to be called 'The Jet Set'). Racing drivers, obviously as big bimbos as the broads who hang around them, are panted over as paragons of sophistication by sports writers old enough to know better; while rugby players are credited with a sort of yeomanish hail-fellow-well-met common sense, their obvious cloddishness thought to be a sign of their gritty blood-and-soil idiot savantism. While boxers – and of all the silly things a man could choose to make a living at, being hit around the head is surely dafter than kicking a ball – are eulogised as noble savage gladiators and credited with all sorts of finer feelings by the high-falutin‘ likes of Norman Mailer and Joyce Carol Oates. They've obviously never seen Frank Bruno in panto. Alone among sportsmen, only footballers are routinely treated like silly schoolboys crossed with prize heifers who have miraculously got their grubby hooves on some serious money. And, like famously melancholic glamour girls – rehab Kate, overdosing Naomi – they must at some level realise that it is humiliating to be valued for one's physical package, like an animal, rather than one's essential, unique self, however handsome the remuneration. Ultimately, anyone who makes their living from their physical gifts, be they supermodel or sportsman, is always aware that they will be considered past their best by the age of 30, giving them another 30-plus years in which to reflect on their glory days. Is it any wonder that they often ask the genie in the bottle to close their eyes with his juniper-scented fingers and make the end come quicker? Whenever I think of footballers drinking, I think of that brilliant poem, 'Killing Time' by Simon Armitage, which goes: 'Red sky at night – shepherd's delight; red sky in the morning – too much to drink again trying to free your mind from the brain it was born in.'

Though the *Daily Mail* may blanch at the idea, the partial turning to drugs and away from drink – though it must be said that it's usually a case of 'and' rather than 'or' – has done much to render modern footballers 'cooler', both culturally and temperamentally, and to stop them from crashing on to the rocks after a few glorious if booze-reeking years at the top as their forebears did.

Anyway, as David Beckham was learning to kick a ball, the first generation of pop footballers were falling like skittles picked on by a particularly eagle-eyed and callous Lady Fortuna, out for a night's bowling with her mates Fräulein Schadenfreude and Mademoiselle C'est la Vie. But to say that their lurid misfortunes helped shape him into the clean and sober young husband he seems to have been forever would obviously be pushing it; for many of his contemporaries, for ever falling out of nightclubs and into three-in-a-bed romps, it is obviously dirty business as usual.

But there always appears to have been some sort of invisible barrier between Beckham, even as a handsome and presumably hormone-charged teenager, and the temptations of the modern world; a cross between a halo and one of those plastic bubbles that hyper-allergic children are forced to live in. His almost obsessional fascination with fashion and with changing his look as often as a hyperactive chameleon seems totally at odds with, and maybe is some sort of gentle rebellion against, his dogged devotion to the moral standards of an earlier time. Born in 1975, becoming a teenager in the late Eighties, Beckham was perfectly placed to be one of the notoriously feral 'Thatcher's Children' who allegedly grew up greedy, hedonistic and oblivious to everything but looking after The Big I Am. But for some reason, give or take a Mohican, a sarong and a thong or three, his personal conduct far more resembles that of the pre-war football champs than the post-war soccer chumps.

In a country where the sole ambition of any decent working-class person is assumed to be to become lower-middle class, it is easy to forget that there was once a distinct English working class that was not also an underclass, which had nothing to do with gymslip mothers, absent fathers and sink estates, and whose values were in fact far closer to

the 'traditional' English idea than those
of the penny-pinching, sexually experi-
mental middle class and the idle,
dumbly promiscuous upper class ever
were. These paragons of generosity,
industry and chastity – a product of
strong unions, a thriving manufacturing
economy and fear of what the
neighbours might say – were particularly
prevalent between the wars and then
after WW2 right up to the destruction of
said manufacturing economy in the
Eighties by Margaret Thatcher. The
alleged moral downfall of the working
class was a direct product of Thatcherite
policies, aided and abetted by her
stooges Major and Blair. Every fatherless
child born to a gymslip mother on a sink
estate can be said to be the fruit of their
loins, the filthy beasts.

But that was yet to come; for now,
David Edward Beckham, known as Ted
(as if in deference to the uniqueness of
his as yet unborn son?), was a gas fitter's

mate and Sandra West was a hairdresser when they married in 1969 in Hoxton, east London, and spent their honeymoon in Bognor Regis before returning to a terraced house in Leytonstone. In this simple sentence we can see a wealth of poignant detail, a snapshot of an age about to pass as surely as that of the steam train: the handsome young couple, both proud of their trades (soon to be outstripped by call centres and McJobs), with high hopes and modest dreams (replaced by low expectations and Lottery fantasies), marrying in a place now overrun with art hags and ponces, holidaying in a thriving seaside town now surviving courtesy of the DHSS, returning to take out a mortgage on a house in an area now gentrified beyond all recognition, and where a terraced house would certainly be beyond the pocket of a hairdresser and a gas fitter – unless it was Oribe and his bit of English rough, that is.

Three children followed – Lynne in 1972, David in 1975 and Joanne in 1982 – spaced with a prudence typical of this careful, clever young couple, and named with the unpretentiousness and modernity of their type. Ancient and modern both; that was the Beckhams, and that is Beckham to this day. 'He was never naughty, except for the time he got his ear pierced at 14 without my permission,' his mother once said. Naughty: even the word smacks of a pre-war childhood.

The presence of a child who from an early age is devoted to something Outside, something Other than the usual dreary hormonal lemming-leap down into the stifling abyss of premature adulthood, can make a family both 'old-fashioned' and strangely flexible. Gifted children, or simply very ambitious ones, to some extent become the 'adult' of their family; not that they become the boss, but their devotion throws into sharp relief the lack of goals that surround them. Paradoxically, their independent desires recreate the family as one from a more old-fashioned age, one with childhood 'hobbies' and pursuits, before the insistent sexualisation of childhood and the full-on pull of peer pressure.

The ambitious child is inclined to 'recruit' their parents to their dream, all the more so as the average teenage peer group regards any hint of enthusiasm or ambition with a level of horror usually reserved for a leper carrying a sprig of mistletoe. You don't have to harbour desires to be a rocket scientist to become a teenage pariah; almost any sort of enthusiasm is regarded as suspect by the pubescent lumpenprole, and even a desire to be a model or singer, let alone something intellectual, can mark a child out (Angela Hayes in *American Beauty*, young Victoria Adams growing up in Hertfordshire). Bullied children are often far more attractive than the norm;

even good looks can be seen as a sign of snootiness, which must be crushed in order to leave the less blessed feeling better about themselves. So the young Beckham's parents became his co-conspirators. His father had dreamed of being a footballer as a boy; now the dream would be passed on, as wealthier families might leave their offspring property or mental health problems. Like all real East Enders, they soon moved to Essex. Much derided by those with more taste than soul, the Essex of the post-war period provided a real chance for cramped and crouched Londoners to stretch their limbs and smile with sleepy surprise at the sheer space and greenery of life. London often seems to be less a living city than a repository of thwarted dreams, and this reason as much as any seems to make it an inappropriate place in which to bring up children: all that stale air, all those lost souls. But for blue-collar Londoners in the Fifties, Sixties and Seventies, the Home Counties often seemed to be one big, benevolent municipal nursery where dreams could grow long legs and run free.

Beckham's ambition gave him a spotlight mind, made him 'tidy' in a way few adolescent boys are. (Shades of the young Lady Diana Spencer saying practically of her virginity 'I knew I had to keep myself tidy for what lay ahead.') Even in his teens he was a great folder of clothes and organiser of cupboards – and as for his virginity, that took care of itself. Although an attractive child, a cute boy and a gorgeous teenager, the young Beckham was quiet and shy. Speech was his second language, perhaps, and the fact that his speaking voice was so unorthodox – maybe the strangest combination of physical perfection and aural mayhem since *Singin' in the Rain*'s Lina Lamont – must have done a great deal to keep it that way. Anyone who was ever a teenager will remember that it was not necessarily the best-looking adolescents but invariably those gifted with the gab who divested themselves of their unwelcome virtue earliest.

But such is the halo effect of Beckham's life in hindsight that it could be argued that even That Voice has worked for him. Without it, the combination of extreme good looks and being so very good at sports might have combined to have made him the Golden Youth of his school, the Prom King, the Boy Most Likely To – and we all know how they end up.

In a fascinating American book published a while ago, called something like *Is There Life After High School?*, a journalist traced a number of Prom Kings and Queens and found that, almost to a man, they were living miserable and unfulfilled lives, having never seen the point in developing their skills and personalities during their balmy reign. It was the geeks and freaks who became CEOs and supermodels. Though the teenage school hierarchy is less savage and stratified here, the syndrome can still be seen. So if Beckham had been blessed with a more mellifluous voice, it is entirely likely that his feet might have failed him; instead, like the Little Mermaid, he was silenced by his own voice and, bit by bit, his feet learned to speak volumes.

By the age of eight, Beckham was scoring a hundred goals over three seasons for his team the Ridgeway Rovers of the Enfield District League; at 11, watching *Blue Peter* (another giveaway to his rather prim, sober childhood self: no hip kid watched *Blue Peter* in 1986), he saw a piece about Bobby Charlton's Soccer Skills Tournament. He won, with the highest score ever, and he won at Old Trafford, the home of the tournament and of Manchester United. The lifelong devotion of Beckham to United – 'There was never another team for me' – handed down from his father, was a source of some puzzlement to his resolutely Southern friends and team-mates. At this time, parallel universe though it may seem, Manchester United was not the beautiful monster it is today, nor even the touchstone team which those who know nothing about football and lots about publicity invariably cleave to. ('Do I support a London team?' said the model Caprice recently. 'Of course I do. I support Manchester United.') Southerners, particularly those in Essex, supported Tottenham (Jews and soulful Gentiles), Arsenal (the chippy and the anti-Semitic), Chelsea (the flash and the sad) and West Ham (the well-meaning and the dim).

Most interesting among these were Tottenham and Arsenal; even their names seemed to blare their opposition, Tottenham Hotspur flamboyant and boastful, Arsenal dour, empire-building

and, well, arsey. Spurs were exotic,
swarthy-foreigner-importing ('In de cup
for Totting-ham!' sang plucky little Ossie
gamely, before the Falklands kerfuffle
took the bloom off the affair) and touchy-
feely (the first football team to hire a
resident therapist, in a milieu where
previously 'therapy' meant having your
ankle wrenched behind your head by
some heaving stevedore posing as a
physio). Arsenal were grim and
determinedly humourless – except when
a savoury little ditty about the alleged
'kike' quotient of Tottenham supporters
seemed too good a chance to pass up.
Those psychos too extreme for Arsenal
could always back Chelsea, where the
presence of Vinnie Jones provided a
natural home; this astoundingly
charmless man, with his mouth like a
little cat's anus, eyes perpetually
watering as though his vitals were being
gripped by an invisible hand, Windsor-
licking ways and Tourretish level of

aggression, personified all that was
rotten about football at this time. While
West Ham, after their Mooreish glory
days, were simply the 'other' London
team; the one that hopeless characters in
soaps and sitcoms – Wicksy from
EastEnders, Alf Garnett – supported.

Before it all went off, before Old
Trafford became a cross between a
catwalk and a rave, an attachment to
Man U – especially coming from a
Southerner – meant something more,
something deeper and stronger and more
than a little sorrowful in its passing. In
the year when Beckham won his
tournament, United was a mess, and
facing the very real threat of relegation
('You're never going to win the League!'
opposing supporters would, incredibly,
habitually chant). To cling to it, as the
Beckhams did, was an indicator of an
inherent moral superiority too deeply
ingrained to want to display itself as
such. It was something about the little

man, something about the indelible
sepia sadness of the Busby Babes dying
as they attempted to continue the
struggle against the Hun by other means,
something about Bobby Charlton forever
on the verge of tears – crying for
England, as well as playing for it – and
something about, however roundabout,
socialism. It was against everything
poncey, flash and sell-out Southerny –
i.e. against everything Manchester
United is today.

Whatever it was, it wouldn't be going
too far over the top – well, just a little –
to say that the boy Beckham felt himself
'promised' to United in the way a boy
prince on the Indian subcontinent will
be betrothed to his bride while they are
both still tiny children. To these ends, he
showed no interest in the ins and outs of
the dating game, and while his friends
put away childish things and chased
girls smelling of Charlie and smashed
ambition, he continued to carry his ball

to the park, serious eyes cast down (though not downcast), dreaming of a mythical and rainy city. When the Manchester United talent scout finally came knocking on the door, and when he signed the contract on his fourteenth birthday, it is fair to say that the last thing this modest young man felt was surprise. On the contrary, he probably felt that he had come home, albeit to a place he had never been. He was, at last, United.

CHAPTER TWO

2 Become 1

Much has been made of David Beckham's alleged dimness over the years – we don't expect our intellectuals to be great footballers, but for some reason we expect our great footballers to be intellectuals. But when it comes to having one's life 'sorted', as the young folk say, he is in a class of his own, considering his youth and his degree of fame. And this in itself bespeaks intelligence. There is a monumentally ill-sorted school of thought which believes that unhappy people are generally 'cleverer' than happy ones, but in my experience the opposite is true; any old procrastinating lump can be depressed, but it takes considerable mental agility, fleetness and flexibility to create, catch and keep happiness, with all the odds against it in this world.

Few people seem capable of combining great public success with a happy private life; usually, something has to give. Those who plough too much energy into their love lives too soon may well find themselves a prisoner of the ever-present pram and Pampers, at the beck and call of their tiny jailer; these will become what Elizabeth Hurley called, with characteristic sensitivity, 'civilians'. Pursue success at the expense of pair-bonding, however, and you are in distinct danger of remaining a narcissistic nonce, loving your opposite number for only as long as they add to your public image. With the vast majority of famous couples, one gets the distinct feeling that they are happy only when there are three people in the relationship: him, her and the photographer. You could never help feeling, looking at pictures of Hurley and Hugh Grant, that for them life without a lens was a life only half led. Following through her train of thought, Hurley probably considers that the opposite of 'civilians' is the rather noble 'soldiers'. But in this instance, I think that 'mercenaries' might be more to the point, as the performing pair's 'love' becomes just another commodity, like sharp cheekbones or a sexy sternum, which they can peddle to the public in order to advance their collective career.

But the Beckhams do not come across like this and, as showy, flash and needy as Victoria is, there is every chance that they could. The reason why they do seem set apart from their rather pathetic, prancing peers is because Beckham's incredible dignity and grace threw that old invisible velvet rope – half bubble, half halo – around first the pair of them, and now, with the gorgeous but unfortunately named Brooklyn, the three of them. Like Daniel in the den of lions – or like a lion in a den of Daniels, if we consider his breathtaking boldness and beauty – he makes the clamour and loutishness of modern celebrity recede, gliding untouched through a scum-tossed sea of thongs, sarongs and unsolicited Adolf Eichmann T-shirts. And if ever his sweet though motor-mouthed wife seems to be in danger of becoming the accidental Delilah to his Samson, he smiles even more sweetly at her, holds her hand extra tight, tells her not to worry because he'd planned a new haircut anyway and on feet of fire takes her with him on his incredible journey. For they are going all the way, to the toppermost of the poppermost, and it's too late to look down now.

The yellow brick road had taken him all the way to his Emerald City, but what David Beckham found there was himself.

He can sometimes seem to have a good deal in common with the Great Oz: a single-minded, meticulous, nerdy little man working the controls of this superhuman spectacle. And as with many people who make it look easy, the secret is that he works twice as hard. Still, you'd think that the most dedicated of 16-year-olds would finally cut loose a little once they were safely out of earshot of their parents, let alone one in a new city, and a place with a vertiginous reputation for hedonism at that. Not that boy Beckham; staying at modest digs, he was happy to be in bed by ten, and when he did go out with the other young United players he would often ask for milk rather than beer. Going out with girls seems to have been something he did, like homework, to keep the peace, pass for normal and buy time for his real love. With women, it was like it was with United all over again; he had the air of being already betrothed, of all that side of things being taken care of, and was content to drift through the meantime in a state of considered euphoria.

The famous have their own form of video dating and introduction bureaux; the difference is that the videos are seen on MTV and the introductions come through model agencies when some new cutie catches the big shot's bloodshot eye. Beckham would never in a million years have dreamed of being so coarse as to call a top agency and ask for the latest model directory, as many pop and sports stars do, sending it back covered with carnal annotations. But in November of 1996, Beckham was abroad on his first game for England, in Tbilisi, Georgia (where, according to Andrew Morton's definitive biography of the Beckhams, he was so awed by the company he had been elevated to that he took along his autograph book – such stunning, almost chilling innocence in such a knowing, worldly world). There, Beckham was to see the video that would change his life. Yes, it was, of course, 'Dancing on the Ceiling' by Lionel Ritchie, when I think I can safely say we all realised that the forces of gravity had gone unquestioned for too long, and that it was our duty as modern beings to challenge this final barrier between us and true freedom of expression. No, I jest – it was, of course, 'Say You'll Be There', the Spice Girls sleek and accomplished follow-up to their first incandescent hit 'Wannabe'. Famously, Beckham pointed at the screen and said to his best friend Gary Neville, 'That's the girl for me and I am going to get her.' He later elaborated, 'It was her eyes, her face. I was sure just from seeing that video, that she was the one I wanted, and I knew that if she wanted me we would be together for ever.'

Beckham's 'simplicity', shall we call it, can sometimes verge on apparent cretinism – see Simba the Lion King, copious tracing of. But equally, statements like the one above can seem almost shocking in their timelessness and resonance. Like the perennial small boy swinging on the lamp post and pointing out that the emperor has no clothes, Beckham can cut through all the modern, relativist cant about romantic love being a con, no one being everything to another person, there being a difference between 'love' and being 'in love' and all the rest of the joyless humbug, to the hard fact that, with the exception of the odd psycho or saint, most of us feel like only half a person when not bonded to a significant other past the age of 18. Dante's vision of the ultimate punishment being that all soulmates are separated from each other at birth and must spend their lives roaming the earth in search of their missing half – the theory that has shaped Beckham's private life – seems far more constant than the penny-ante witterings of the counselling cowboys and therapy quacks about the inadvisability of co-dependence and the desirability of keeping one's own interests. The 'Say You'll Be There' video was an action-chick movie spoof featuring the girls capering around the Mojave Desert dressed as flagrantly cheesy caricatures of male fantasy. (For a change!) Victoria, dressed in a black PVC catsuit, was Midnight Miss Suki, a rather mild-mannered dominatrix whose sadistic repertoire was largely composed of pouting, pointing and prancing. What was it about her that so cried out to Beckham, we can wonder, when Baby might have seemed a more suitable playmate? It's just possible that he might have realised that she was at that time actually very much like him – a lovely bit of state-of-the-art machinery hiding a rather lonesome, driven outsider. At the same time as Alpha Male saw Alpha Female, looking over their respective shoulders might have been Squeaky Beckham, the schoolboy with the silly voice, and Sticky Vicky, the solitary student teased about her livid acne; it was a double date, so to speak.

When the sports hero and the pop star did finally meet, Squeaky and Sticky were at hand to screw it up for them; Victoria had also been nursing a mild crush on him, and went to see him play against Chelsea; they waved at each other in the players' lounge afterwards, but were too shy to take it any further. It was left to the Spice Girl to walk it like she talked it; next time she saw him after a match, in the players' lounge at Old Trafford, she walked right up and told him how good he was; 'As soon as she smiled I knew everything was going to be okay.' Even Squeaky and Sticky must have cheered.

And the rest was hysteria. You'd think there'd never been a Heterosexual

Human Couple before, that it was something completely new and totally freakish, as though we'd previously been going around practising troilism or marrying horses. No one, it seemed, could take their eyes off them. But what was really surprising was how much hatred they attracted, from otherwise apparently intelligent, enlightened people. Two gorgeous young creatures, wildly in love, independently rich solely by their own efforts in totally harmless professions, attracted a level of vicious loathing which never faced the ridiculously over-privileged Charles and Diana, the frankly homicidal Bonnie and Clyde and the notoriously minging Antony and Cleopatra. Why?

This was when I began to get really interested in the Beckhams; when I realised that they were a spotlight turned onto the poisons of others. They are a pair of beautiful social barometers, lithe litmus tests who highlight the sad failings and desires of their critics. Between them, they have inadvertently managed to reveal more about the plagues of sexism, snobbishness and plain old-fashioned envy that disfigure Blair's Britain than Germaine Greer, Dennis Skinner and Snow White's wicked stepmother put together. When people criticise the Beckhams, they generally say – in the words of the old American Express ad – more about themselves, all of it bad. Who criticises Posh for being too thin? The same commentators who jeered at the modestly luscious curves of Baby and Sporty Spice when snapped in bikinis. Who slams the Beckhams for greed and ostentation? Not socialists, who really do believe in wealth distribution, or those who spend their lives working selflessly for others, but money-grubbers who are bitter about never achieving their dreams of avarice. It's the same old sour grapes decanted into a shiny new bottle: class hatred, a long wail of petulance from middle-class salarymen who can't understand how a gas fitter's son came to be living la dolce vita while they themselves scrabble gracelessly for cash and have to scrape by with two holidays in Tuscany a year. Posh and Becks, on the other hand, were brought up to believe that effort and application alone bring rewards, and that received pronunciation and a solid education are neither here nor there. Despite her nickname, there is nothing Posh about Victoria; she was given the name solely because, in contrast to Scary, Sporty and Ginger, she was 'ladylike'. 'Easy V doesn't come for free/She's a real laydee' mocks Geri in 'Wannabe'. And she was the only watchable thing in the risible *Spiceworld* film, constantly sending up her image of vacuous fashion victim – 'Shall I wear the little Gucci dress, the little Gucci dress or the little Gucci dress?' (She also has the great populist gift that anything she wears, no matter how costly, she makes look as though it came straight off the rail at Top Shop; no wonder the little girls love her.) Her father (called 'Tony', of all the gloriously common names) is a self-made man who passed on his belief in the virtues of graft and perseverance to his daughter, who wears her ancient assumed handle with the same good-natured resignation as the grown-up Baby or the subdued Scary. Only an idiot would think she meant it; cue Naomi Campbell asking 'Why do they call you Posh?' It says a lot for Victoria's good upbringing that she didn't widen those huge chocolate-drop eyes even further and ask innocently of the sour-faced supermodel, 'I don't know – why do they call you beautiful?'

In fact, one of the appealing and interesting things about the Beckhams is that he, a football player from Essex, should be common but seems so aristocratic while she, with her tarty clothes, turned-up nose and Estuary squawk, is so delightfully common. They compliment each other completely, but not in the predictable way – bit of rough wins uptown girl – that you'd first think.

We don't hate the Beckhams because they have loads of cash and spend it ostentatiously; the Queen of England, who is supposed to stand for all that they lack, rides in a gold coach and wears jewels on her head so heavy that they make her neck ache. That's ostentation, if you like, that's greed – and we're paying for it! – no matter how many pieces of string Her Maj saves and how many electric lights she turns off: all the better to keep you safely in the dark, my forelock-tugging tribe!

No, I believe that those who hate the Beckhams do so because they so very obviously made it all by themselves. We pay lip-service to meritocracy, but its rare reality disturbs us, makes us aware of our own idleness or bad luck – and of course, idleness can be a form of extreme, long-distance bad luck. The inherited rich, like the Windsors, or showbiz dynasties, like the Redgraves, or public-school boy wonders, like Branson, we can handle – oh, it was the old boy's network, it's not what you know but who you know, they were born with silver spoons in their mouths. We know that they didn't make it fair and square, from scratch, at the same starting line as the rest of us, and that perversely comforts us. But when we regard a pair of young people who have achieved vast wealth (she has a fortune of £24 million, he has £5 million) from nothing – not from sponging off a spouse or waiting for a parent to die, not by trading off a famous name or good connections, never surprised in shame or compromise, a law unto themselves – we are forced to face our own busted dreams, and it hurts. This is why Victoria attracts so much more ire than, say, Jade Jagger or Tara Palmer-Tomkinson, both patently the sort of people who would have been Nobodies all their lives had they not had the luck to be connected to Somebodies. It's also why the Beckhams – who never took a penny from the public that wasn't willingly proffered – take so much more stick, incredibly, than the cretins who have recently run everything from British Airways to the railways to the Dome into the ground, only to be rewarded with vast six-figure golden handshakes from public funds.

The Beckhams are also hated because they have shown up the prevailing, pathetic sexism of our society, the bankruptcy of the whole big man-little woman model of marriage and the lie that Alpha men are naturally promiscuous. All this is inadvertent, of course. They would be the first to admit that they are not intellectuals, unlike most of the bimbos from Prince Charles to Bono who pass as such these days. But the Beckhams do, in a very unique way, upset our precious notions of what the 'natural' limits to an equal relationship between the sexes should be. We were just getting used to laughing off 'New Man' as a pathetic, stay-at-home wimp bullied by some burly ball-buster of a bitch, and returning to the safety of the old lies like 'All women love bastards', when along came the obviously virile, wildly successful Beckham and the ultra-feminine, delicate Victoria to turn this vicious and damaging cliché on its scabby head.

Still, it is strange how these youngsters, so well-matched and mutually adoring, anger people so much more than the other sorts of celebrity couples who make up the soft parade of modern sexual fame. A beautiful girl on the arm of a wrinkled old git old enough to be her grandad? Fine. A man who trades in his wife for a new model every decade? Swell. A footballer who beats up his wife or girlfriend, often in front of their children? Give the guy a gong! A successful, beautiful young man who clearly worships his successful, beautiful young wife and their son? GET AWAY, YOU DISGUSTING WIMP! Sex is behind a lot of it, of course. That the Beckhams take such an obvious physical delight in each other must be very galling indeed to the balding, softening fortysomething male journalist whose sex life started to slide years ago.

At the risk of sounding like a perve, you can tell what successful sex they have by their wonderfully slippery sexual personae; only a man painfully aware of his own sexual shortcomings will feel that he must play the dominant male at all times, and only a sexually dysfunctional woman would ever want to be seen as a coy little flower. Shortly after their marriage a remarkable collection of Annie Leibovitz photographs of the couple appeared in *Vanity Fair*; the single most striking impression was not of the rather Grand-Guignol-meets-Disneyland interior of their much-mocked mansion 'Beckingham Palace', but of the extent to which they both confirm and flout our ideas of beauty and gender. Yes, Victoria is small, delicate and dainty, but she is also (in the pictures, and at her best) dangerously dark and crop-haired as a boy, with eyes that flash like Heathcliff's. Yes, Beckham is tall, muscular and fit, but he is also blond as a favoured baby, with light eyes that wince away from conflict and a voice like a teenager's, barely broken. ('Barely Broken' could be the Beckhams' epitaph.) His is an almost Garbo-like frozen facial perfection, the jawline and cheekbones apparently worked out by the Great Artificer with spirit level, slide rule and graph paper; that he is hung like a horse doesn't hurt a bit – not one iota! – either.

In the most striking image of all,

Beckham lies surrendered across a huge Gothic table, his arms flung out, his head back, his eyes turned towards the camera in something that looks like shame until we look harder and see – with a soupçon of shock – that it is in fact pure, perfectly passive relish. For above him, as if just about to fuck him, crouches Victoria, her feral glance at the camera one of utter possession and triumphalism. But it is no more triumphalist than the passive Beckham's; together, as a team, they look like nothing less than a pair of arrogant, sun-kissed young lions about to go at it with a vengeance. In a sentence which revealed far more about his own fears and fantasies than it did about Beckham's supposed unmanliness, a *Daily Mail* journalist wrote tremulously of 'David draped submissively across the table, averting his eyes from Victoria's dominant stare'. In fact, the look in his eyes says, 'Yes! Result! Look what I've got crawling all over me – she's richer, older, cleverer than me! I give in, totally – and don't you wish you had what I've got?' It is a classic image of beauty and desire untrammelled. Of course it upsets people.

It didn't help when the birth of their son made them even stronger, when the patter of tiny trainers leaves most couples drained and de-sexed. But in a way it was totally predictable that this most golden of young working-class males would take to fatherhood with the grace and suppleness of a dolphin to water and group sex. In recent years sociologists – the rotten snobs – have been shocked to discover that blue-collar men actually spend far more time with their children than their professional contemporaries, and feel far less threatened by the gains of feminism. (This is probably because, as D.H. Lawrence pointed out a long time ago, the working classes are surer of themselves sexually.) When I see Beckham carrying his little son on his shoulders on the pitch at Old Trafford, offering up his mouth in an exaggerated pout for a kiss while the tot leans down to bestow one, I am reminded of my own working-class father who, though so violently offended by effeminacy that he left the room swearing every time Lionel Blair appeared on TV, resolutely took me to see my beloved Bolshoi Ballet every time they appeared at the Bristol Hippodrome, hiring a box, no less, and reading his racing paper all the way through. Working-class men make natural fathers in a way that other men, obsessed with status and career advancement, just do not. In the famous Athena poster of the muscled young navvy type cuddling the baby, or in Beckham's relentless beauty, never more complete than when looking at his son, we seem to see all that men could be – that toughness and that tenderness combined without conflict or cruelty – if they only stopped trying to control everything so much, if they stopped worrying for five minutes about looking soft.

Far from rending his marriage, Beckham's experience of fatherhood seems to have extended his patience and forbearance even further, strengthening a union already both companionate and passionate. Perhaps the secret is that he is, in fact, the real grown-up, the strong silent husband to a wife who can be exasperating and monumentally indiscreet. 'At the moment I'm looking after my two babies,' she gushed to a magazine last year. 'David might look grown up, but he needs a lot of looking after.' Then, shamefully, there was the repeated shriek of 'Do you think David's an animal in bed?' to a baying gay male crowd as she sought to promote her first solo single at a nightclub. He wears her knickers, don't forget, and she says, 'I am a strong woman, and David does a first-class job of being a father. Overall he is the perfect house-husband. He does more housework than I do and cooks more often than me.' The casual observer might also venture the opinion that David does a first-class job of keeping his cool when his private life is used as a fast-track superhighway for his wife's addiction to mainlining headlines but, hey, it works for them.

There is a book by Amy Bloom called *Love Invents Us*, and when we look at Posh and Becks, if we are the least bit sensitive, we will also see the lonely girl bullied because of her bad skin and the shy boy silent because of his strange voice who, through sheer will and belief, became a pair of beautiful swans (the chosen bird on their specially designed coat of arms, with, shamefully, a crown and, understandably, the words LOVE AND FRIENDSHIP), each perfect in the light of the other's eyes. If they have formed a hard, glistening carapace around themselves and their world, who can really blame them? They've been hurt enough. But unlike so many other snivelling sport'n'showbiz neurotics, they have chosen to heal each other, to keep it tidy.

The Beckhams have had the last laugh, and are still having it large. Behind the silkscreen of their success, they are the Revenge of the Nerds turned King and Queen of the Prom through some fantastic alchemy of fame, love and money. Feared by the sour, loved by the sweet, the shy boy and the lonely girl are at last having their day in the sun. And only a churl would not wish them all the luck in the world.

CHAPTER THREE

Too Much

But on the other hand . . . it would take a funnybone of stone not to smirk at their antics occasionally.

That wedding – and those thrones! That coat of arms! To add insult to injury, the swan was the wrong way round and the initials of the yappy couple were V & D! That mural on poor Baby Brooklyn's wall of Posh and Becks, bless 'em, tarted up as Prince Charming and Cinderella! It is often hard to countenance their lifestyle, even as their greatest supporter, without feeling the overwhelming desire to adopt a Lady Bracknell accent, look down one's lorgnette and intone 'A mural?'

It was said of Fred Astaire and Ginger Rogers that he gave her class and she gave him sex. Sometimes, with the Beckhams, it seems that she gives him crass and he gives her hex; their coupling, while bringing them massive added punch publicity-wise, has also brought with it ceaseless public ridicule. But then, it is unlikely that the love antics of any of us would stand up to public inspection, as the annual sick-fest that is the Valentine's Day personal columns bears witness. It is easy to conclude that the Beckhams have more money than taste – but with a combined income of £8.2 million p.a. For the Beckhams, every day is Valentine's Day – make of that what you will. Come on – which joker at the back yelled out 'Yeah – tacky, commercialised and mercenary'?

To some extent, they make part of their living simply by being in love. They are cheerleaders and ambassadors for heterosexuality, as Charles and Diana,

Andrew and Fergie, Edward and Sophie were intended to be. And of course the Beckhams are preferable, partly because the fee they command for displaying their sexual orientation so ostentatiously is not prised from the public pocket via the civil list, but, rather, willingly offered up by the readers of *OK!* magazine, and partly because they can actually stand to be in the same room as each other. But it is an interesting paradox that these high priests of heterosexuality are then the campest act since Liberace; in a perfect world they would both be secretly gay, and their wedding the widest, wickedest wink imaginable to their secret legions of worldwide compadres.

It's interesting that these days we associate low-key, bland taste in decor with intelligence, whereas historically the smartest people were often the most flamboyant − a lively mind requiring more in the way of entertainment. As Clough Williams-Ellis, the brilliant architect of Portmeirion put it: 'I would rather be a little vulgar than boring – especially to myself.'

Whatever, on 4 July 1999 – a suitably purple and apocalyptic choice – David and Victoria (both blessed with the names of famous monarchs, look! – Queen Geri and King Robbie just don't have the same ring) sat on twin red and gold thrones in a castle in Ireland, surveyed their empire and found it good. It was indeed a magic kingdom that the Beckhams reigned over that day; among a verdant decor of dark green and purple, vaguely based on the Disney version of Robin Hood, they entered to the strains of the *Beauty and the Beast* theme and started the dancing to *The Lion King*. Luckily, there was no urchin hanging from a lamp post, as he might have asked why the happy couple didn't just book a week at Disney World Florida and have a full character breakfast to celebrate their special day.

It is fun, if only briefly, to try to imagine how the Beckhams' brains work. Do they know what they are doing, as they often claim, and are having a laugh at the expense of those who tut over their 'bad taste', making them style guerrillas of a kind in a world tyrannised by the bland flat-pack oppression of Habitat and Ikea? Or did they only get wise after the event and invent this alibi in order to deflect further mockery, as when poor Dolly Parton started saying gamely in every interview, 'It costs a lot of money to look this trashy!'? Considering Disney products to be as elegant and romantic as they do, was there ever a time when – sometime during the fourteen months it took to put the whole extravaganza together, maybe at the end of an extra long day when logic gets fuzzy and everything seems possible – they actually considered having someone dressed up as Mickey Mouse, say, in attendance? Donald Duck conducting the service, perhaps, with Simba the Lion King himself as Best Man? It's mad, but how much madder, on your wedding day, than entering to the music from *Beauty and the Beast*? And more urgently, which was supposed to be which?

But hey, you pay, you play. It took half a million pounds to rig the castle up as Sherwood Forest; Victoria's tiara (borrowed, not bought) was worth £100,000 and her dress £60,000. But as the couple would be getting a cool million from *OK!* for the exclusive rights to the wedding, they'd still be seeing a profit. It remains a minor irony that *OK!* is the respectable tip of an iceberg of a pornography empire owned by one Richard Desmond, friend and benefactor of pure-souled family man Tony Blair. By paying this most respectable and monogamous of couples a million pounds for a series of fully-clothed photographs (as opposed to the usual fifty quid to some Asian babe, or grandma), he completely contradicted the idea that sex sells more than anything else. By keeping themselves pure for the big day, the Beckhams had pulled off a coup that left the most expensive practitioner of the Sex-For-Sale racket standing.

But let's not lose our sense of perspective here (she said hurriedly, having done just that). Just as we don't pay footballers to be great intellectuals, the same goes double for being wild-eyed leaders of the People's Revolution. The Beckhams were products of post-political Blair's Britain, a system that can only be described as Socialism For The Rich, Red Raw Capitalism For The Poor. Under this novel regime – and don't forget that during Blair's reign the gap between the richest and the poorest in this country became the biggest ever, exceeding that of even the Thatcher years – millionaire shareholders of Railtrack were handed vast tranches of taxpayers' money while the people forced to use the trains – or hospitals, or schools – faced a Third World level of incompetence and squalor. If the Labour Lord Chancellor feels happy spending half a million pounds of public money on wallpaper and stuff, it seems a bit rich to pillory a sports star and a pop singer for spending £10,000 of their own on a gazebo.

The Beckhams' money washes in and out in great waves of foaming, furling cash, soaking them in radiant slo-mo and splashing the rest of us with specks of chilly irritation. Though most of their fortune was earned by her, most of the new money comes from him. In their early days it is fair to say that the Spice Girls were not backward in coming forward when it came to sponsorship deals, and after a certain saturation point their stock couldn't help but go down.

But Beckham has played a long, slow game, and rather than aim to have his image plastered frantically over every lollipop, scrunchy and disposal camera, he has chosen his deals with deliberation and discretion. Brylcreem seemed a suitable choice, with its echoes of a saner time which Beckham still seems spiritually bound to; a million-pound deal with Police sunglasses made sense, what with all those flashbulbs going off. And while the Spice Girls seemed to pursue their commercial quarry, pushing and squealing like a posse of preposterous cartoon creatures, he just stands there on some stage or podium and turns his fine, noble face to face the clamours of capitalism – and it flows all over him, leaving him clean and unmarked. Curiously, it is on occasions to commemorate his commercial co-option that Beckham can look his most saintly and pure, wide clear eyes welcoming the cameras gladly; he looks like a magnificent child – or perhaps the Minotaur the moment before it went mad, proud of its splendid freakishness.

It is all well and good to make a song and dance about how much footballers earn; the only problem is that, logically, it makes no sense. It is romantic but wrong. Every penny they take is given gladly and voluntarily – as with pop singers and all other entertainers – as opposed to the vast sums of public money squandered by Government, usually in order to make the rich even richer. How can a society which produced the Dome ever pillory the Beckhams? Of course, the catch is that in their infancies, both football and pop music – as opposed to, say, tennis and acting – made unspoken covenants with their disciples in the early days that it was, now and for ever, Us against Them. This feeling persisted well into the Sixties and Seventies, but with the explosion of the entertainment market in

the Eighties, it could no longer stand up
to even the briefest of inspections. It was
inevitable, of course; any situation
composed of love object and adoring
audience can never be anything but
savagely hierarchical by nature. And just
as Labour and Conservative politicians
have far more in common with each
other, despite their ceaseless taunting
rhetoric, than they do with any of their
voters, so the most apparently out-
rageously opposed entertainers – Arnold
Schwarzenegger and the Manic Street
Preachers, say – have more in common
financially, morally and spiritually than
they do with their fans. There was
always Them and Us; only it wasn't a
question of the straight and rebellious, or
the old and young, or the poor and rich.
It was only ever a case of those who are
paid to entertain and divert us from our
life on earth, and those of us who are so
desperate to be entertained and diverted
that we are prepared to make very rich

indeed the people who can manage to do so. Think about this: those who we will count upon to save our lives – doctors and nurses – will be paid in a year what a major league footballer – who exists only to divert us from our lives – earns in one day, or a week at most. What's all that about?

Pop dealt with its co-option into the system decades back and even learned to revel in it – in a stroke of almost incredible greed masquerading as playful showmanship, David Bowie is now also (only?) a bank, with his own credit card and everything. After all, 'selling out' has two meanings for a pop group, and they now sound equally attractive. But football and its fans are still trying to come to grips with what has happened. One day it was about little boys kicking a ball between jerseys for goalposts in the street, the next day it was about little boys bankrupting their parents as the swinish Premier League changed their strips with each new season. It's not surprising that there's a few 'issues' kicking about there, a bit of the old 'conflict' in need of 'closure'.

It's globalisation, of course; those that got shall get, those that didn't shall lose. For all its ills and disappointments, the Soviet Empire did stand as a sort of dam against the excesses of capitalism, with its eternal boasts of a home for all, work for all and tube stations so clean you could eat your dinner off the floor. Once it was gone, it was Liberty Hall; the law of the jungle, moderated during the first nine-tenths of the 20th century, suddenly became all the rage. From now on, only the strongest would survive – and the weakest would pay through the nose for the privilege of watching them play.

In football, this had several effects. The Bosman ruling allowed players to swap clubs with ease, chasing the biggest offers and leading to massive salary inflation. In 1992 the Premiership League was started, a separate universe attracting huge sponsorship money – around the same time as extraterrestrial television bid massively for live games, wiping out the BBC and leading to the eventual annihilation of – sob! – *Match of the Day*. (Now and for ever, that irritatingly cheery theme tune will have the same ability to evoke copious weeping in grown men as Lorraine Ellison's 'Stay With Me, Baby' does with their girlfriends, which showcases an interesting set of diverging priorities, to say the least.) The top teams now make around £25 million each year, every year, for their annual television rights. Admission to Premiership games has soared from £1 or under for First Division matches in the Seventies to around £25; it now costs more to spend an afternoon at a Premier League game than it does to spend an evening at the

Royal Opera House. Manchester United takes more than £1.4 million every time it opens its gates.

The FA milked the understandable desire of TV to show live Sunday club games and Cup competition matches between the likes of Arsenal and Man U – or, to give them the new names so proudly emblazoned on their shirts, between SEGA and SHARP. The huge sums they came away with went straight into the players' pockets – with just the loose change being spent on improving ground safety and facilities. In 1979 the first £1 million player was created; in 1988 the £2 million mark was breached. Then in 1996 Alan Shearer went from Blackburn to Newcastle for £15 million, and in July 2001 Juan Sebastian Veron signed for – guess who? – Manchester United for a staggering £28.1m.

In keeping with the tenets of globalisation, the maximum rule on foreign players was abolished; history was made in 1999 when Chelsea became the first British club to field a team containing not one home-grown player and, very often, their captain Dennis Wise would be the only Brit in the starting line-up. In a lovely twist on the long tradition of foreign workers being brought in to do lowly paid jobs that the English think beneath them, overseas footballers began fetching up here in the Nineties when the domestic variety got too expensive – 'Play for Man U for £50,000 a week? You're 'aving a laugh, aintcha, mate? Go and get some dago to do it!' Of course it cuts both ways, though; refused £130,000 a week by Tottenham, Sol Campbell was promptly offered £200,000 by Barcelona – preferring eventually to cock a snook at Spurs by signing with their old rivals Arsenal for a mere £80,000.

The EU, never backwards in coming forwards when it comes to widening the gap between rich and poor – see its surreal farming subsidies, which created a minority of millionaire farmers alongside a wretched, ruined majority – stuck its oar in with a surprising overhaul of the transfer system, under which a player would be able to break his contract after three years by giving only three months' notice, suffering only four months' suspension if he downed tools earlier. Beckham, who had been negotiating for a £100,000 a week contract before this ruling, was suddenly in a position to demand twice that. This development even put the wind up the bigwigs of the Premiership clubs, who had previously seemed as happy as pigs in muck, frankly, to roll cheerfully in the golden dross of deregulation; the Arsenal vice-chairman David Dein called the new rules 'disturbing'. Disturbing – this, from a man who habitually and of his own free will stands in an enclosed space with tens of thousands of Arsenal fans!

Beckham's annual £2 million pay-packet looked set by the summer of 2001 to go up to ten, a piece of news which must have had a good part of the chief hawkers of the luxury goods market down on their knees weeping Swarovski crystal-type tears of joy. For another thing that David Beckham does extremely well, apart from play football, is spend. He does it with the effort-lessness of a leaping dolphin and the homing instinct of a Stealth missile. Boy, can he spend. Victoria can sometimes display the penny-pinching savvy (if you want to be polite; stinginess, if you don't) of the born and bred middle classes (albeit self-made, in her parents' case), dropping £14 on little tops from the likes of 'Tarts', a Hertfordshire boutique (you always feel that 'selling' their wedding and various other private moments was more her speed than his, too; these prudent, pennywise bourgeoisie, you see). Beckham, on the other hand, has taken to serious money with all the elan and verve of the proletarian pools winner – i.e. as near as dammit as we have left to an old-fashioned, blow-it-all aristocracy. But whereas they spend their unearned legacies on heroin and houseboys and end up dead of AIDS at 40, this golden child glides on wheels of steel, shimmering in a heat haze of wealth, sliding it effortlessly into goals all along Bond Street and Brompton Cross.

No celebrity has ever seemed so untouched by money as Beckham does, yet so infinitely commercial. It both slides off him and sticks to him – he is Teflon Boy and Tar Baby both. It's his Zen-like calmness that gives his numerous deals dignity; he feels he has done nothing in any way wrong by flogging Brylcreem or Adidas or sunglasses, and so his absolute innocence transmits itself to us, as full-on and straight as his smile, through his eyes and his body language, be it on the pitch or leaving the Ivy. (Unlike Victoria, who can often seem darty, hunched and frowny – rather furtive, like someone guilty of an unseen crime. Or perhaps, more to the point, like someone who seems to feel that they've been Getting Away With It for a long time, and may be rumbled any second now.) He is the opposite of all those famous 'edgy', 'credible' American actors who make television ads only to be seen in Japan, and in doing so actually draw more attention to the prostitution of their 'art'. Unlike these showbiz hip-ocrites (hep-ocrites?) who do their business with Mammon furtively and thus, para-doxically, make it a far dirtier business than it otherwise would be, Beckham speaks boldly of his and shares our sheer amazement that one man can be worth so much to so many. 'I am aware of myself as David Beckham the brand. It's very weird,' he told *The Face* in the summer of 2001. 'I was driving through London the other day and I looked up and I was on the back of a big red bus and I'm thinking, "What's that all about?"' I'm good, comes the still small voice, guilelessly, good in every way a man can be good. So how could anything I do ever be bad?

At worst, his love of shopping could be seen as shallow. But it really does seem to be the lesser of the evils that performers of all kinds are prone to rely on to fill that audience-shaped hole when not doing what they were born to – drinking, drugging, eating disorders or that ultimate self-indulgent and narcissistic addiction, therapy. He shops in a very masculine way, too, it must be said, with none of the edge of desperation and hysteria that afflicts many an It Girl. If Gary Cooper had shopped till he dropped, he'd have shopped a lot like Beckham.

Why does he make everything look so dignified? Why isn't he a buffoon like so many of his Premiership peers, forever falling out of Sugar Reef and Attica and on to the front of the Sunday papers, fists flying, feet flailing and ego in overdrive? I think it's a bit like the Raymond Chandler line about a man having to go down these mean streets who is not himself mean; someone must walk through the Valley of the Shadow of Shallowness who is not himself shallow – just to prove, just once, that fame doesn't have to be a mask that eats the face, and that great wealth and fame actually can, if the character is strong enough, leave body and soul unbroken.

Beckham's face, as he leaves Brown's and Red Cube time after time, is remote and serious and satisfied, somewhere between a saint going to the stake and the cat that got the cream. His hand is in Victoria's – and she is probably frowning and looking at the ground and pretending that she doesn't really want her picture taken – but his mind is

elsewhere, you feel. It's running endlessly across a deserted playing field,
chasing a ball, the wind whipping
around its 12-year-old face, its feet
already so skilled and accomplished that
they appear to be joined to the ball by
some invisible cord. The Beckham
caught in the glare of the flashbulbs,
solemn in a sarong or bejewelled like a
popinjay in a pair of £20,000 diamond
and platinum hoop earrings is the decoy,
as is the one driving too fast in the BMW
X5, the Ferrari Maranello, the Lincoln
Navigator or the two Mercedes; the
perfect stranger who protects the
brilliant little boy forever running across
the suburban field, haunted by the
spectre of his own imminence, waiting
to be born.

CHAPTER FOUR

Holler Holler

A couple of years ago the young
Bermuda-born footballer Shaun Goater
of Manchester City urged the FA to warn
Millwall FC that they could be shut
down, after a 1–1 game throughout
which he was ceaselessly barracked by
fans of the London side. 'It wasn't just
adults – it was kids too, and you just
wonder what they are going to grow up
into,' said the dignified young man
afterwards. Every time he went for the
ball, the ape noises started (the irony of
Millwall fans, of all people, accusing
other people of being the Missing Link
was not lost on those of us who have had
the pleasure of their company, but

anyway) and when City scored the equaliser, a mass of Millwall supporters streamed on to the pitch, showing the restraint and faith in their team's ability to win fairly that we have come to know and love. 'The message was clear,' Mr Goater told John Edwards of the *Daily Mail* afterwards. 'The last thing we wanted was to score a winner. It sounds ridiculous, but that is how scared we were.'

The idea of a black boxer, in the closing years of the 20th century, being scared to land the winning punch, or of a black team being frightened to win at rugby or cricket, though, is surreal; only football provides a breeding ground for this germ culture. Football fans seem full of a non-specific rage, which it is hard to reconcile with the simple, childish act of kicking a ball between goalposts. As someone said in a negative review of *The Vagina Monologues*, 'If I wanted to hear 50,000 people yelling "Cunt!", I'd go to a football match.' If football makes them so cross, why not go swimming instead?

One would really have to be working overtime at being a caring, non-judgemental person for it not to occur to one, however briefly, that there is something very gay indeed about football fans; not gay in a good, healthy, out-there kind of way, but gay in a closeted, self-loathing, woman-hating sort of way. The recent inclination of the players themselves to advertise shampoo – silky locks leaping up in slo-mo – kiss each other in the manner of paramedics attempting mouth-to-mouth resuscitation and generally ponce about, cannot have done anything to cool the eternally frustrated ardour on the terraces either. When Saturday Comes, a hell of a lot of lads go home with hard-ons.

It is largely to do with the homoerotic desire of the fans for the players, I believe, that the players' wives are now so routinely and filthily abused. And the chosen accusation of 'Taking it up the arse', which is invariably meted out to Mrs Beckham, probably stems from the fact that a good number of the geek chorus dream of taking it exactly that way from the beautiful Mr Beckham – ooh, he looks so rough with his hair like that! Mmm, with all that soy sauce running down his manly chest – yummy! And with the charming chants which advocate the desirability of the Beckham baby dying of cancer – 'And you just wonder what they are going to grow up into' – this thoroughly unhealthy, not to say sick obsession with football's ultimate golden boy has come to a festering head.

You need only look – go on, just for a moment, you won't necessarily lose your lunch – at the likes of Baddiel and Skinner to see that sexual retardation and love of the Beautiful Game go hand in clammy hand. At 15, a boy should put aside childish things – like ball games –

unless he can make a grown-up living out of them, and start chasing girls. If he doesn't put one aside firmly enough, he tends to neglect the other with disastrous results. (Painful, too; a recent study in Italy found an alarming tendency to grow deformed testicles in boys who played too much football.) Show me a man who loves football, and nine times out of ten you'll be pointing at a really bad shag.

Of course, this doesn't necessarily apply to the players themselves, who are as cavalier with their gifts (see high incidence of drinking and drugging) as the naturally talented ever tend to be. The professional player gets it both ways, being paid to do what he loves and then becoming a top-totty magnet. But the football lover who can't make the grade has to get a real job – a dull, low-paying job, as often as not. And he certainly won't have Posh, Louise and Caprice queuing up to go out with him.

Is it any wonder he feels such eye-watering envy for the very players he adores?

The problem – such as it is – is that no British football player has ever before scored so high as Beckham in every department. Gascoigne was a 'genius', if you will, but he was also ugly, violent and couldn't stop weeping, except to compulsively rearrange his bath towels. Best was a handsome genius, but he was an alcoholic. And even Bobby Moore was forever followed, after Mexico, as if by some particularly sparkly ball and chain, by that diamond bracelet. These flaws, weaknesses, whatever they were perceived as through the perverse prism of fan-love, helped cancel out the feelings of resentment which might otherwise have blighted their careers, too. At the end of the day, it was possible to feel sorry for them, and therefore not to feel inferior to them.

You can't feel sorry for Beckham, no

matter how you slice it. Go on, try it; say 'I feel really sorry for David Beckham' out loud. Did it sound convincing? Thought not. Let's look at the list. Completely realised ambitions? Check. Millions of pounds? Check. Brilliant marriage to beautiful woman? Check. Masculine first-born, nice house, pair of Dobermann dogs, representation as demi-god in golden Buddhist shrine in Thailand? Yes, yes, yes, yes! It's like the conveyor-belt finale at the end of *The Generation Game* – Beckham goes home with the lot, and the lovely hostess, too. And to add insult to injury, that skin-tight leather catsuit also hinted that he's packing a foot – and it ain't got toenails.

Envy and thwarted sexual desire make for an explosive cocktail of emotion – and, of course, Beckham presented the mentalists with the perfect platter on which to demand his lovely head even before the royal wedding and its attendant excess. The occasion was the

World Cup, the date, 30 June 1998, and
the dainty dish was served up courtesy
of Beckham's achievement in becoming
only the second England player ever to
be sent off during a World Cup match.
Talk about blaming the victim. And it
would have to have been against
Argentina! But the reaction of the
England fans, and of a vocal minority of
the country generally, spoke volumes
about the level of loathing that had been
gradually building up against Beckham.
England were on top when the
Argentinean (obviously still sore about
losing that little knockabout in the South
Atlantic all those years ago) knocked
Beckham over; the Argentinean then
pulled Beckham's hair as he lay on the
ground. It was a nasty, catty, underhand
gesture, and must have snapped the
serene self-control which had stayed
strong through so many years of jibes
and jeering from his own countrymen,
who had always seemed more offended

by a football player who used conditioner than by a football player who regularly hit his wife. (Boxing is a sport where men beat up men; football is a sport where men beat up women.) Beckham kicked out, barely touching his tormentor, and was sent off. The ten-man England team lost.

There's a telling photograph of the incident: the referee holds up the red card while Beckham, long-haired and wearing white, gazes up at it as if transfixed by something magical. Around him, a group of short-haired Argentineans, clad in black, smirk and sneer, like a group of yobs passing a lone female on the street. You can't help thinking that there is, as with the ever-fuming fans, some element of frustrated sexual desire in the scenario. Whatever, it was open season on the golden boy. Effigies were burned, acres of newsprint devoted to this monstrous devil-spawn and police protection brought in for the first time, and it never really went away. An Islington butcher put two pig's heads in his window, one labelled DAVID, the other VICTORIA.

Great sumptuous waves of loathing greeted him wherever he went, at home or away, for Manchester or for England. The charming chants about his son hopefully dying of cancer revved up in earnest; it was this one which finally drove him – oh, menace to society! – to raise one dignified middle finger to the England fans during the Euro 2000 match against Portugal. It was deadly serious, but beautifully restrained; so cool, calm and collected, so to the point, so much the opposite of the running sore of spite that poured from the mob.

And mob and media alike reacted as though he had run amok with a machete through the stands. The defaced newspaper photographs of Brooklyn customised with fake bullet holes and blood, the kidnapping threats, the stalkers, the real bullets with Beckham's name on – there was a palpable feeling that, by having it all, Beckham deserved everything he got.

The jokes are the most interesting thing, though – not the nastiest thing, not like the chants and the threats, and not the most surprising thing, like respectable senior politicians doing the same stuff, in joined up writing, as the terrace hate mob. But they are interesting for what they say about the people who tell them, and about how little we have moved on in our attitudes about class and gender since the middle of the last century.

The jokes are told by men, invariably, but not obviously ignorant, snobbish, sexist men. They've been to university, they're anti-racist and they mostly came up moaning on about 'Fatcher'. But they find two things about Beckham really, really funny, endlessly amusing. And these things are a) that Beckham is of working-class origin and has a funny voice (i.e. not like theirs) and b) that Beckham is married to a woman more intelligent and forceful than him. I know – isn't it a hoot! Almost as funny, almost as tragic, as the underlying belief behind Beckham jokes that the only reasonable, credible, non-funny thing to be is a middle-class man who bosses his wife around. There are no jokes about those from the likes of Rory McGrath and Sasha Baron Cohen.

It's the gang mentality of these jokers that is so sad; the playground bully agreement that there are just two designated victims, and only they will get the kickings. It gets so monotonous, apart from anything else, so safe, so lacking in spice and surprise. I personally find, say, Lenny Henry and Dawn French hilarious: I'd love to hear some jokes about them. But then, she's educated and he makes his wife look stupid in the Sunday papers. They're not funny. (Least of all when they're trying to be, heh heh.) They're 'normal'.

It hasn't really stopped, the hating. It followed Beckham across the centuries, even. In January of 2000, admittedly idiotically, the Beckhams attended the controversial Tyson boxing match in Manchester. Before it started, the MC announced the presence of various celebrities in the crowd. When the spotlight finally fell on them, the crowd went wild; the air was electric blue with obscenities, jeering and abuse. They attracted two classes of hatred, even: that from the cheap seats, and that from the adjacent VIP boxes, many occupiers of which simply stood up and screamed insults into their faces. Then they sat down, these solid citizens, to cheer on a convicted rapist. It's almost brilliant in its preposterousness.

And as late as April 2001, Beckham told his wife to stay away from the

England match against Finland at Anfield, as he was worried about her safety. It obviously wasn't the inscrutable Finns Beckham was expecting to cut up rough, still sore about some busted treaty struck with Perfidious Albion in the 18th century. No, it was the England 'fans' he was wary of – those strange little men who still haven't had anything happen in their alleged lives to dim the memory of a summer's day three years ago, when a man pulled another man's hair and got a swift kick in return. The poet wrote about 'the private massacres going on behind the eyes' of the mildest-seeming citizen in the street. Regarding Beckham and the emotions he provokes in so many, this seems less like poetic licence and far too much like reportage for comfort.

CHAPTER FIVE

Viva Forever

Someone else will come along, of course, eventually; the lonely crowd will lose its collective imagination to some other bright-eyed boy with less baggage and a more winning way. Wings on his feet, head in the clouds, the works. But Beckham'll keep it for a long, long time. If his aim is true, maybe longer than any ball-kicking holy fool from this damp, dazzling little island, ever. Maybe he'll be the best ever at what he does! – and which one of us could wish for more?

She won't help matters, though. Without the ballast of her girl gang, Victoria won't age well; her nervousness and neediness will start to seem like neurosis, pure and simple, as she approaches the outer suburbs of youth. Her slenderness will become stringiness, her spiritedness spite. There have been signs of it already, the corrosion of her character; that was a spectacularly nasty bit of business, her and an acolyte singing 'Who Let The Dogs Out' when the sad glamour girl Jordan walked into the players' lounge at Old Trafford. The bullied bullying, the nerd turned nasty – and in the very place where her love story started, too. Sticky Vicky probably hung her head and cried.

She's forgotten Sticky Vicky, most likely, up there in that rarefied air, where memory is hazy and pain seems somehow . . . spoilsport. The glinting of the Beckhams both may have started already, of course, depending on whose story you believe. 'I'm a gay icon, I'm a gay icon', Victoria has claimed her husband prances around saying, while he rallies with the rather cool rebuke in

The Face (or as near as he'd ever get to it, bless him): 'People say icon and it's a bit embarrassing for me to talk about; I don't turn around to Victoria and say "Good morning, I am an icon."' Glinting: that lovely word coined by the great social commentator Peter York, to describe that sad but almost inevitable moment when the beautiful, dumb, differently abled performer discovers that the plain, clever, book-learned types are talking about them – and is ruined for ever, always reaching too high and never regaining their initial spirit and soul. It happened to Madonna, Schwarzenegger, Robbie Williams, Geri Halliwell; only a few bounce out the other side, self-mocking and marvellous, like George Michael and Kylie Minogue. Respectable critical acclaim is the Bluebeard's Castle of the lively artist, and peeking into its rooms, though tempting, may hold the agent of their destruction. Be bold, be bold, but not too bold . . .

But see what I've done? I've classed Beckham as an entertainer, a pop tart, a flimsy thing. Such is the paper-wraps-stone power of glossy covers, velvet-covered thrones and flash haircuts over flesh and sinew and a child born to mortals with a gift for kicking a ball so extreme and true that it looks like actual magic. But of course sportsmen, especially footballers, no matter how many starlets and stunnas they date, how many nightclubs they fall out of, how many suits they model, will always be the exact opposite of showbiz kids, where sleight of hand and size of eyes is everything, and talent only a Plus-One. Substance is all for the sportsman; the simplicity of goals scored, games won, battered and bruised hearts lifted aloft for just one more working week.

There may well be trouble ahead because, at the end of the day, while Victoria may have bound her young lion king tightly to her side by dazzling his beautiful eyes with lovely things and playing on that inarticulate but strong side of him which yearns still with all the force of a sensitive, non-academic, working-class boy child for the 'creative', the 'artistic' as an escape from the life lived in the soul-destroying job and on the settee, he is not in the least like her. She must know, if she is in any way aware of the milieu she operates within, that over the next five years she will totally outlive her usefulness to the little girls who look up to her. As kids must reject their parents' influence on the way to becoming their own people, they must go on to reject the influence of their idols in order to finally reach the shore of self-realisation. It's fair to say that the parents generally take it better than the idols do.

Contrary to the cliché, there isn't really a thin line between love and hate – if there was, we'd all go round having mad pashes on traffic wardens. What there is, is a thin line between love and indifference; with star-love, the line is naturally crossed quicker. It's always been so, but it moves faster these days, due to both the sheer candour of the love-objects and the increasing boldness of the media. Just think; in the opening steps of the 21st century, upon becoming interested in an attractive, famous stranger, we will probably know more about them – their childhood traumas, their wildest fantasies – in the space of two weeks than Victorian spouses came to discover about each other over two decades. And the most important piece of knowledge we will acquire, the moment before we dump them and put away childish things for ever (that, or turn into a stalker) is that they were only ever in it for the money, every time. They were, literally, living off us, as surely as if they were strutting gigolos; they were, as all stars are, gold-diggers. There was no 'relationship' at all, even at that moment when we ran upstairs weeping, slamming the door on the amazed faces of our long-suffering parents, crying out that NOBODY UNDERSTANDS! except Freddy and the Furies, or Vicky and the Vomits. They were only ever in it for the money.

But it's different for boys, for good or ill. Though I've poured scorn on sport in general and football in particular all through this book, even I can understand that the impulse which binds the football fan to his team is in another league altogether from the passing hormonal whim which binds a pop fan to her crooner of choice. Usually this restraint is admirable; at the height of their opposing passions, Duran Duran fans never once attempted to seriously mutilate or murder Spandau Ballet fans, even though lines like 'I am beautiful and clean and so very, very young', 'With a thrill in my heart and a pill on my tongue' and 'She used to be a diplomat, but now she's down the laundromat', not to mention the general vocal performance of Mr Tony Hadley, might have wangled a suspended sentence on the grounds of extreme provocation.

The putting away of pop heroes is a thoroughly sound testament to the pragmatism and progressiveness of women. But the relentless, often joyless loyalty to football teams speaks volumes about the pride and prejudice of men; the same pride and prejudice that once brought civil rights and trades unions into being. In an age so frighteningly free of conflicting ideology – 'The End of History', as the American historian Francis Fukyama celebrated the collapse of communism – and a world so seamlessly re-serfed for the convenience of the global corporations, the very fact of not agreeing looks like intelligence, however stupid the insults. It is the essential dissent of sport, combined with the unspinnable ability of the players, which gives it a purity and excitement that mere entertainment – the opiate of the people, who now have *Friends* instead of friends, and *Neighbours* instead of neighbours – can never have.

He loves his Posh, we know he does. That's so much of why we like him. Though often touted as a prime example of 'New Man', Beckham reminds me of so many working-class men I knew when I was growing up in the Sixties and Seventies: physical workers, gentle giants, faithful husbands to women who were volatile, bossy and shrill and therefore, in this gorgeously contrary logic, dizzy little ladies who must be allowed to have their way because to stand up to them in any shape or form would mark one out as that most ludicrous of curiosities, a man who argued with women! Call it patronising, call it what you like; all I know is that my father and his factory-worker friends, with their soul-deep sense of male superiority, behaved with oceans more forbearance and courtesy (albeit bemused, followed by a good shared smirk with one's mates down the pub afterwards) towards women than your typical educated and enlightened middle-class modern male – terrified that his soft, pen-pushing job makes him a sissy – ever could.

Without wishing to be vulgar and personal – oh, go on, then! – it is obviously Beckham's sexual confidence that has kept him so singularly sane and happy. After all, talent couldn't do it for Maradona, Best or Gascoigne, all of whom, like Beckham, came from loving and supportive homes. In a rare occurrence, Beckham the man has grown up at the same rate as the sports hero, and much of this is due to the obduracy and determination of his wife, chosen with such shy determination for the qualities she would bring – beautiful

Midnight Miss Suki, with the long, long legs made to keep on moving and the big, big eyes made to focus on her goal. But very soon, the time will come for the head of the household – not elevated by his gender, but by his talent – to put the brains of the operation in her place, and make her realise that while she plays a short, sharp game well, he's in it for the duration; folk history, at least.

Sven Goran Eriksson will be his next Significant Other; the new manager of England, worth some £2 million a year for the next five years, has the qualities in spades that Beckham needs in a mentor to move on to the next stage – the main stage, when he steps away from the slight, steely shadow of Miss Suki. Courteous, calm and cultured, he will bring, by virtue of his foreignness in general and his Swedishness in particular, a healthy balance and remove to the relationship of the England manager with his golden children, a relationship which in the past – founded in ties of blood and soil, no less! – could get just a little clammy and hysterical, and was probably not conducive to the best and most logical football. That jocko-homo stuff – 'Thirty years of hurt! Never stopped me dreaming! AND NOBBY DANCING!' – isn't going to play with Eriksson, who will put his team together as objectively and pragmatically as an Ikea flatpack. He has so little time for prima donnas, apparently, that he dropped one player from his previous team Lazio just 20 minutes before a big game for complaining that his top was too tight. So he won't take any nonsense from the fashion plate in the Number 7 shirt.

So far, it has been Beckham's good fortune that he has had Victoria to save him from the bad influence of football; in the future, it may be that he will need football to save him from the bad influence of Victoria. She saved him from the yobbery and misogyny that taint the modern game; she should finish her good work by not insisting that he stay the showbiz poltroon, the demon lover cover boy, the straight man half of the ultimate celebrity couple. Because increasingly, they can seem as isolated and deranged as any other showbiz drones; the idiocy of going to the Tyson fight, when so many had protested about the convicted rapist being allowed in to Britain in the first place, was compounded by their attendance, in February 2001, at an Eminem concert in Manchester. All well and good, if foul-mouthed, fag-baiting, trailer-park Demon Kings are your thing – i.e. if you're 15 – but, after previously calling the sewer-mouthed soubrette 'very talented', Victoria and her husband walked out looking absolutely amazed and devastated. A friend told the *Evening Standard*: 'They were just so disgusted that they had to leave; they said that they thought it was terrible that Brooklyn would have to grow up in a world in which Eminem was a star.'

One does not have to be a fan of the ludicrously over-compensating (white, slight, lisping) rapper in order to be delighted that he had seen fit to accidentally outrage the prim sensibilities of Mrs Beckham by allegedly taking drugs, wielding a chainsaw, riding an inflatable ten-foot-long penis and pretending to die in 'Ol' Sparky'. Furthermore, I bet Baby Brooklyn would have been absolutely delighted by such over-the-top pantomime – 'Mummy, why's that man sitting on that big snake?' And it begs the question: exactly which Eminem records had the lovely couple (reported to be great hip-hop enthusiasts) been listening to before their rude awakening? Not the ones the rest of us heard, celebrating rape, queer-bashing and drug-guzzling, obviously, but a special celebrities-only underground album, perhaps, extolling the simple pleasures of monogamy, shopping for his'n'hers outfits in Brompton Cross and tracing drawings of Simba the Lion King for one's own true love. Bless.

In April 2001, Manchester United won their seventh championship in nine seasons; Beckham had been with them for five of those. This, remember, after that dry season which had lasted from 1967 until 1993. And so, incredibly, though appearing to the rest of the surly world to have all the sensitivity and humility of a decathlon-winning billion-aire wife-beater, Manchester United still consider themselves in some part of their collective consciousness as being the Little Guy Who Made It, and Beckham personified their wide-eyed and blissful ignorance when he exalted, 'The feeling of excitement is just as great as when I won my first trophy, and I don't wish to sound greedy but I'm not satisfied with my collection yet.' But what will happen to this sweet-natured superman when the thrill finally does go – or is he simply so Zen that it never will? My feeling is that his surprising and appealing purity of intent and continuing lack of ennui is linked vitally with the almost mystically fated union with United, and that if he ever leaves them he will suffer the fate of the hero's squeeze in James Hilton's *Lost Horizon*, crumbling to nothing in front of our eyes. Though the amount of money he would go for would be huge, any move would cheapen him.

But he may do it in the end, go to a London club, in what he will believe is a bid to be his 'own person', but which will really be about the fact that Victoria insists that they live near her family, and that the constant bombing along the motorway back and forth between Manchester and Hertfordshire, as he has been doing for three years now, is really no way to spend your one and only life.

117

Though no one is suggesting that a married woman should be prepared to up sticks and follow Her Man wherever the fancy takes him ('Carrying the pots I've made, following behind me!' as the old Four Tops song had it), there is something strange and almost unwholesome in the fact that Mrs Beckham would rather her husband knock himself out commuting to his rather physically demanding day job than distance herself too far from the bazaars of Bond Street. Having achieved a perfect marriage, both companionate and sexual, and silenced all the fools who decree that Alpha Male can never curb his polygamous animal instincts, she now seems intent on proving that a woman given equality in a relationship will inevitably seek the upper hand, and in the process reduce her soulmate to a doormat. Funny; Beckham's unworldly parents never hesitated in letting their beloved only son follow his Northern star far away from home when he was just a boy, but his wife, worldly and wily, and you'd think flexible in matters of career and ambition, must have him to hand, right on her patch in the Home Sweet Home Counties. Perhaps, in the end, even after all this time, it's a class thing; his working-class parents, with nothing to give him but their love, loved him enough to let him go, so that he could become himself. But his wife – the petit bourgeoisie, the demi-Posh – grew into her class, and ended up knowing the price of everything and the value of nothing. Does she ever wonder what he thinks about on those long, lonely journeys from North to South and back again? Probably not. Which would make her the truly Scary Spice.

It has been said that when people stop believing in God they believe not in nothing, but in anything. And in our increasingly secular society, where sport has become the altar before which crazed penitents fling themselves effing and blinding in search of grace, the shy boy with the clever feet surely carries a heavy burden on those silky shoulders.

He has not yet been asked to walk on water or turn Evian into Red Bull, but in the summer of 2001 it was announced that Beckham would lead a £14 million campaign to persuade tourists terrified of foot-and-mouth disease to return to Britain. Due to the various ineptitudes of farmers and Government alike, there had been a 21 per cent fall in foreign tourism, losing the country – called in one German newspaper 'The Leper of Europe' – some £2 billion in revenue. Optimistic estimations said it would take at least five years to return tourism to its former level. To coincide with the start of the football season, under a £2.8 million deal with the Premiership, images promoting Britain were to appear at the start and end of matches, to be shown in more than 100 countries and seen by more than 160 million people. 'Beckham has already pledged his support and the BTA is negotiating with his agent,' reported the *Sunday Times.*

You had to laugh; a simple lad with a gift for kicking a ball was now expected to turn around the fortunes of his sad, sick country, where the sons of the soil and the men at the top had failed completely. It was like some mystic medieval morality play: the innocent power of the idiot savant saving the day, when the puffed-up pretenders had finally admitted defeat. And it is perhaps the defining image we will keep of David Beckham when we look back at the opening steps of an already depleted and dismayed new century; dignity under pressure, decency in decadence, true talent amid the putrefaction of publicity – in a sad and shimmering time, a world in freefall, when everything melted into air and we never did find our way home.

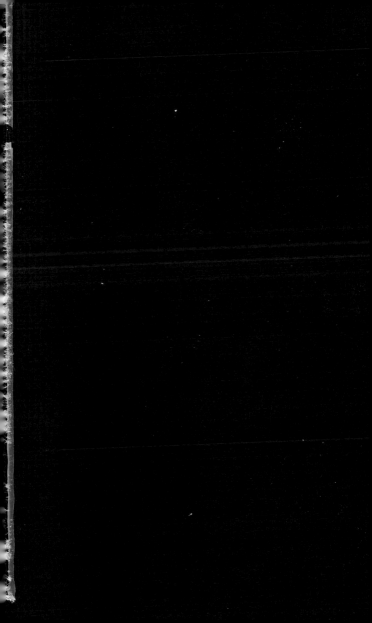